CAMOUFLAGE

The Hidden Lives of Autistic Women

DR SARAH BARGIELA

Art by Sophie Standing

JKP

LONDON AND PHILADELPHIA

ACKNOWLEDGEMENTS

·

This book is dedicated to the autistic women I
interviewed, without whose openness in sharing their
experiences, this book would not exist.

THIS BOOK WILL INTRODUCE YOU TO THE
EXPERIENCES OF AUTISTIC WOMEN – AN
INTRIGUING AND LITTLE-KNOWN SUBJECT WE ARE
DISCOVERING MORE ABOUT EACH DAY.

HERE'S AMY. SHE'S A JOURNALIST WHO WAS
DIAGNOSED WITH AUTISM, AGED 20.

BEFORE GETTING A DIAGNOSIS, SHE SPENT A
LOT OF TIME RESEARCHING AUTISM ONLINE.
AFTER HER DIAGNOSIS SHE DECIDED TO SET UP
A FORUM FOR OTHER AUTISTIC WOMEN – A PLACE
TO ASK QUESTIONS, UNDERSTAND AUTISM AND
SOCIALISE. SHE'LL BE OUR GUIDE THROUGHOUT
THIS BOOK.

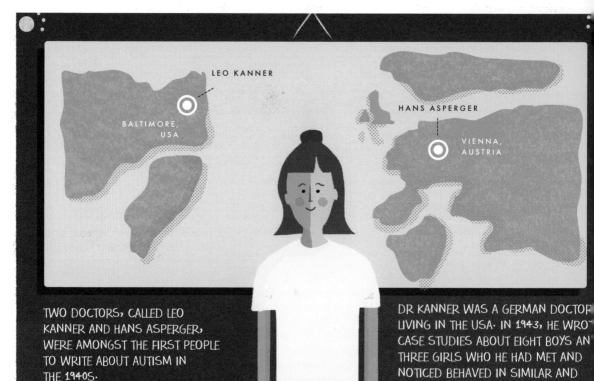

TWO DOCTORS, CALLED LEO KANNER AND HANS ASPERGER, WERE AMONGST THE FIRST PEOPLE TO WRITE ABOUT AUTISM IN THE 1940S.

DR KANNER WAS A GERMAN DOCTOR LIVING IN THE USA. IN 1943, HE WROTE CASE STUDIES ABOUT EIGHT BOYS AND THREE GIRLS WHO HE HAD MET AND NOTICED BEHAVED IN SIMILAR AND UNUSUAL WAYS.

ONE OF THE LITTLE BOYS WAS CALLED DONALD. AT THE AGE OF 4, LITTLE DONALD HAD AN EXTRAORDINARY MEMORY FOR FACES, NAMES AND SONGS THAT HE HAD ONLY HEARD A FEW TIMES, AND HE WAS HAPPIEST WHEN PLAYING ALONE.

A YEAR LATER, IN 1944, AN AUSTRIAN PAEDIATRICIAN CALLED DR HANS ASPERGER[1] WROTE ABOUT FOUR BOYS HE HAD MET IN HIS CLINIC. HE NOTICED THAT ALL FOUR BOYS WERE ONE-SIDED IN CONVERSATION AND ALL OF THEM HAD A SPECIAL INTEREST. HE CALLED THEM 'LITTLE PROFESSORS' BECAUSE THEY COULD TALK ENDLESSLY ABOUT THEIR SPECIAL INTEREST.

ALTHOUGH BOTH KANNER AND ASPERGER RESEARCHED AND WROTE ABOUT AUTISM[2] THROUGHOUT THEIR CAREERS, THEY NEVER ACKNOWLEDGED EACH OTHER'S FINDINGS.

perger syndrome is named after Dr Hans Asperger.   2 The word autism comes from the Greek 'autos', meaning 'self'.

IN THE 1980S, STUDIES OF GIRLS WITH AUTISM EMERGED. IN 1981, A PSYCHOLOGIST CALLED LORNA WING FOUND THAT PEOPLE DIAGNOSED WITH 'HIGH-FUNCTIONING' AUTISM WERE 15 TIMES MORE LIKELY TO BE MEN AND BOYS, RATHER THAN WOMEN AND GIRLS. WHILE IN 'LOW-FUNCTIONING' AUTISM, THE RATIO OF MEN AND BOYS TO WOMEN AND GIRLS WAS CLOSER TO 2:1.³

HIGH-FUNCTIONING AUTISM

15 x

LOW-FUNCTIONING AUTISM

2:1

3 The terms 'high functioning' and 'low functioning' are considered by many in the autism community to be unhelpful. In the autism research literature, 'high' a 'low' functioning are used to refer to individuals with average/above average and below average IQ. However, it is argued that a person's level of functioning solely defined by their IQ but is instead dynamic and dependent on context. For example, someone with a high IQ might become non-verbal in a stressful situat

SO, WHY ARE THERE FEWER WOMEN AND GIRLS DIAGNOSED WITH AUTISM COMPARED TO MEN AND BOYS?

NEUROTYPICAL

AUTISTIC

1. THE 'EXTREME MALE-BRAIN' THEORY

SCIENTIST SIMON BARON-COHEN PROPOSED 'THE MALE BRAIN IS WIRED TO SYSTEMISE, THE FEMALE BRAIN IS WIRED TO EMPATHISE'. SO BEING AUTISTIC IS A BIT LIKE HAVING AN EXTREME VERSION OF A MALE 'SYSTEMISING BRAIN'.

2. GIRLS ARE BETTER AT HIDING AUTISM

RESEARCHERS TONY ATTWOOD AND JUDITH GOULD SUGGESTED THAT AUTISTIC GIRLS ARE LESS LIKELY TO GET DIAGNOSED BECAUSE THEY ARE BETTER AT HIDING AUTISM WITH 'SOCIAL MIMICRY' SKILLS.

. THE FEMALE AUTISM PHENOTYPE IS DIFFERENT O THE MALE AUTISM PHENOTYPE

UTISTIC FEATURES ARE EXPRESSED IN DIFFERENT VAYS IN AUTISTIC FEMALES AND MALES. FOR XAMPLE, WHILE AUTISTIC WOMEN ARE GOOD AT YE CONTACT, AUTISTIC MEN ARE LESS SO, LEADING O THE IDEA OF A FEMALE VERSION OF AUTISM OR EMALE AUTISM PHENOTYPE'.⁴

4. QUESTIONNAIRES USED TO DIAGNOSE AUTISM DON'T CAPTURE FEMALE AUTISTIC FEATURES

QUESTIONNAIRES USED TO DIAGNOSE AUTISM HAVE MOSTLY BEEN VALIDATED ON AUTISTIC MALES, SO THEY MIGHT NOT BE SENSITIVE ENOUGH TO PICK UP FEATURES THAT ARE ONLY PRESENT IN AUTISTIC FEMALES.

otype: inherited chunks of code (genes) that make us who we are, for example the genes for our height.

ype: what we see as a result of the interaction between our inherited (genetic) code and our surrounding environment.

CURRENTLY, AUTISM IS DEFINED AS:

'DIFFICULTIES SINCE CHILDHOOD IN SOCIAL COMMUNICATION AND INTERACTION AND RESTRICTED, REPETITIVE BEHAVIOURS OR INTERESTS.' [5]

SOCIAL COMMUNICATION AND INTERACTION

MEANS ALL THE THINGS RELATED TO SOCIAL SITUATIONS, LIKE BEING ABLE TO START CONVERSATIONS OR READ PEOPLE'S FACES FOR THEIR EMOTIONS…

5 This definition of autism comes from the American Psychiatric Association *Diagnostic and Statistical Manual for Mental Disorders*, 5th Edition (DSM-5).

RESTRICTED INTERESTS

THIS IS WHERE SOMEONE WHO IS AUTISTIC MIGHT BE INTENSELY 'INTO' A PARTICULAR ACTIVITY OR TOPIC, LIKE LEGO, A TV SERIES OR HORSES. THEY MIGHT ALSO HAVE INTERESTS THAT ARE MORE UNUSUAL, LIKE DOOR KNOCKERS OR ROCK FORMATIONS OR KITCHEN UTENSILS.

IT MIGHT EVEN BE A SUBJECT THAT LOTS OF PEOPLE LIKE, FOR EXAMPLE DOGS. HOWEVER, THE MAIN DIFFERENCE IS THAT AN AUTISTIC PERSON WHO LIKES DOGS IS LIKELY TO HAVE AN ENCYCLOPEDIC KNOWLEDGE ON ALL THE BREEDS, SIZES AND VARIETIES, COMPARED TO SOMEONE WHO JUST SAYS THEY 'LIKE DOGS'.

REPETITIVE BEHAVIOURS

REPETITIVE BEHAVIOURS INCLUDE
REPEATING WORDS OR PHRASES,
KNOWN AS 'ECHOLALIA'…

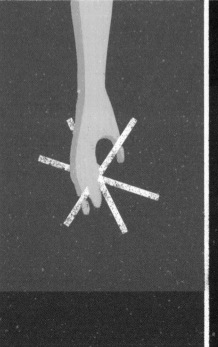

…OR REPETITIVE HAND OR BODY
MOVEMENTS LIKE SPINNING
SOMETHING IN YOUR HANDS OR
ROCKING YOUR BODY…

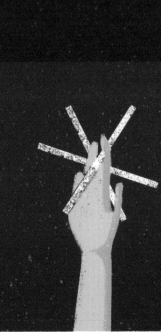

...OR INSISTING ON THE SAME DAILY ROUTINE. FOR EXAMPLE, ALWAYS EATING THE SAME THINGS FOR BREAKFAST...

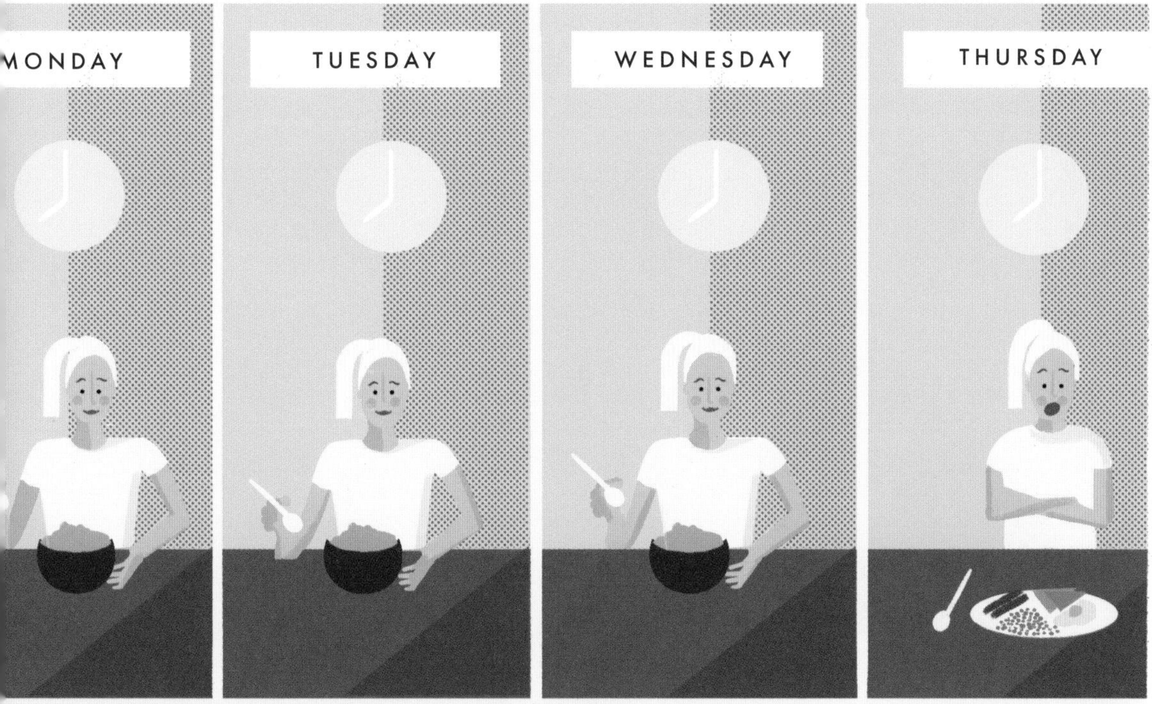
MONDAY
TUESDAY
WEDNESDAY
THURSDAY

...OR TAKING THE SAME ROUTE TO SCHOOL OR WORK...AND FINDING IT OVERWHELMING OR UPSETTING IF THAT UNEXPECTEDLY CHANGES.

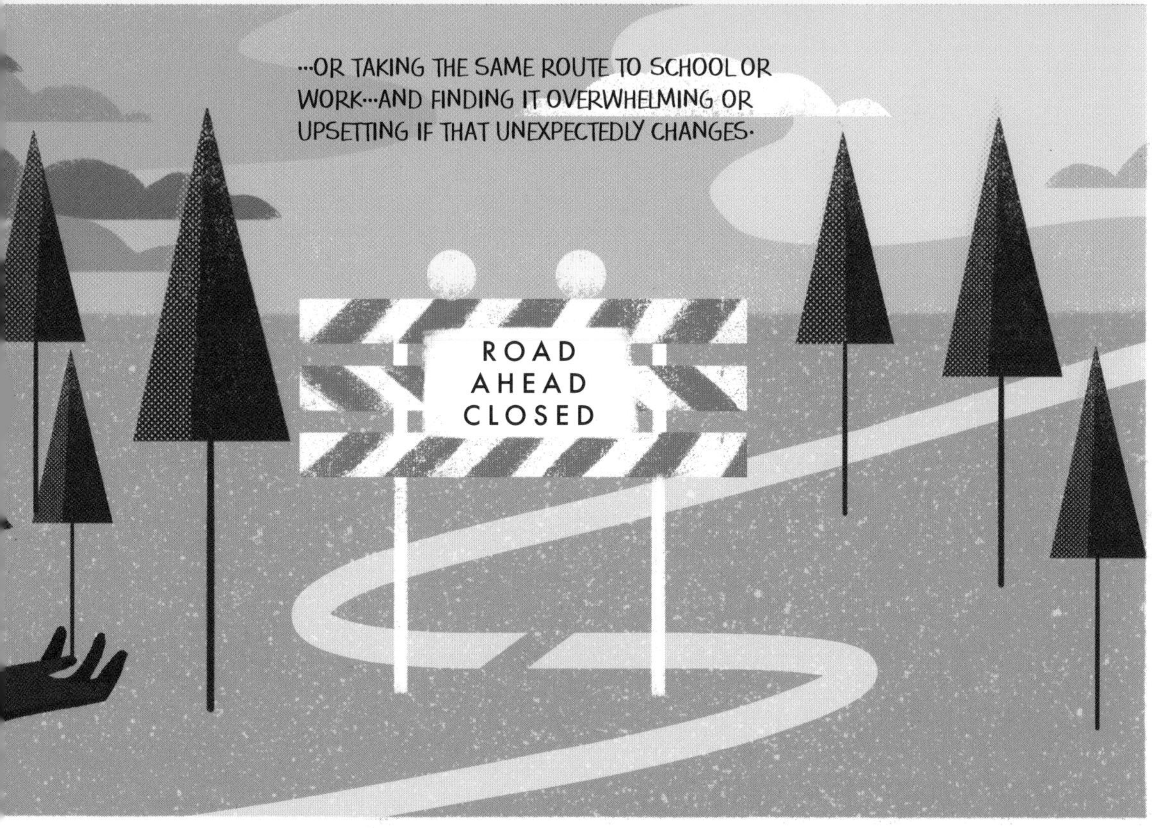
ROAD
AHEAD
CLOSED

SENSORY SENSITIVITIES

OFTEN, REPETITIVE BEHAVIOURS ARE ABOUT REGULATING, SEEKING OR AVOIDING SENSORY INPUT.

SENSORY MEANS ANYTHING RELATED TO YOUR FIVE SENSES. EVERYONE REACTS DIFFERENTLY TO CERTAIN SENSATIONS, WHETHER YOU ARE AUTISTIC OR NOT. FOR EXAMPLE, SOME PEOPLE WORK WELL WITH LOUD MUSIC, OTHER PEOPLE NEED TOTAL SILENCE.

BUT THE RANGE OF SENSITIVITY FOR SOMEONE WITH AUTISM IS MUCH WIDER AND RANGES FROM HYPER-SENSITIVE (SENSORY AVOIDING) TO HYPO-SENSITIVE (SENSORY SEEKING).

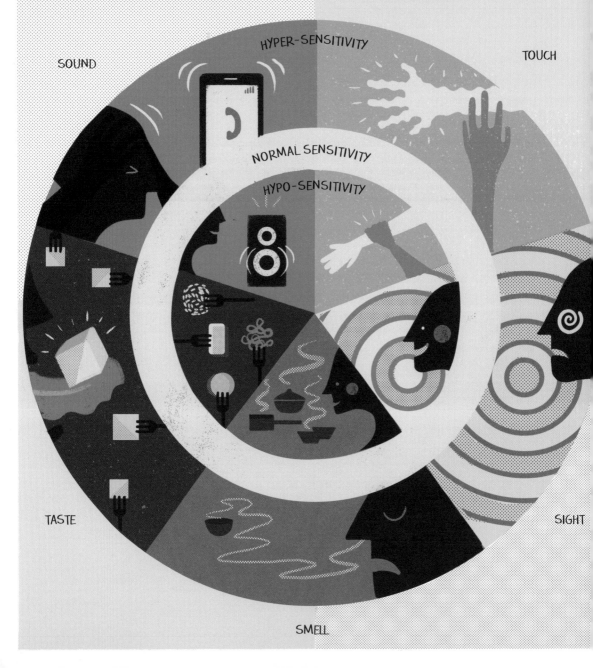

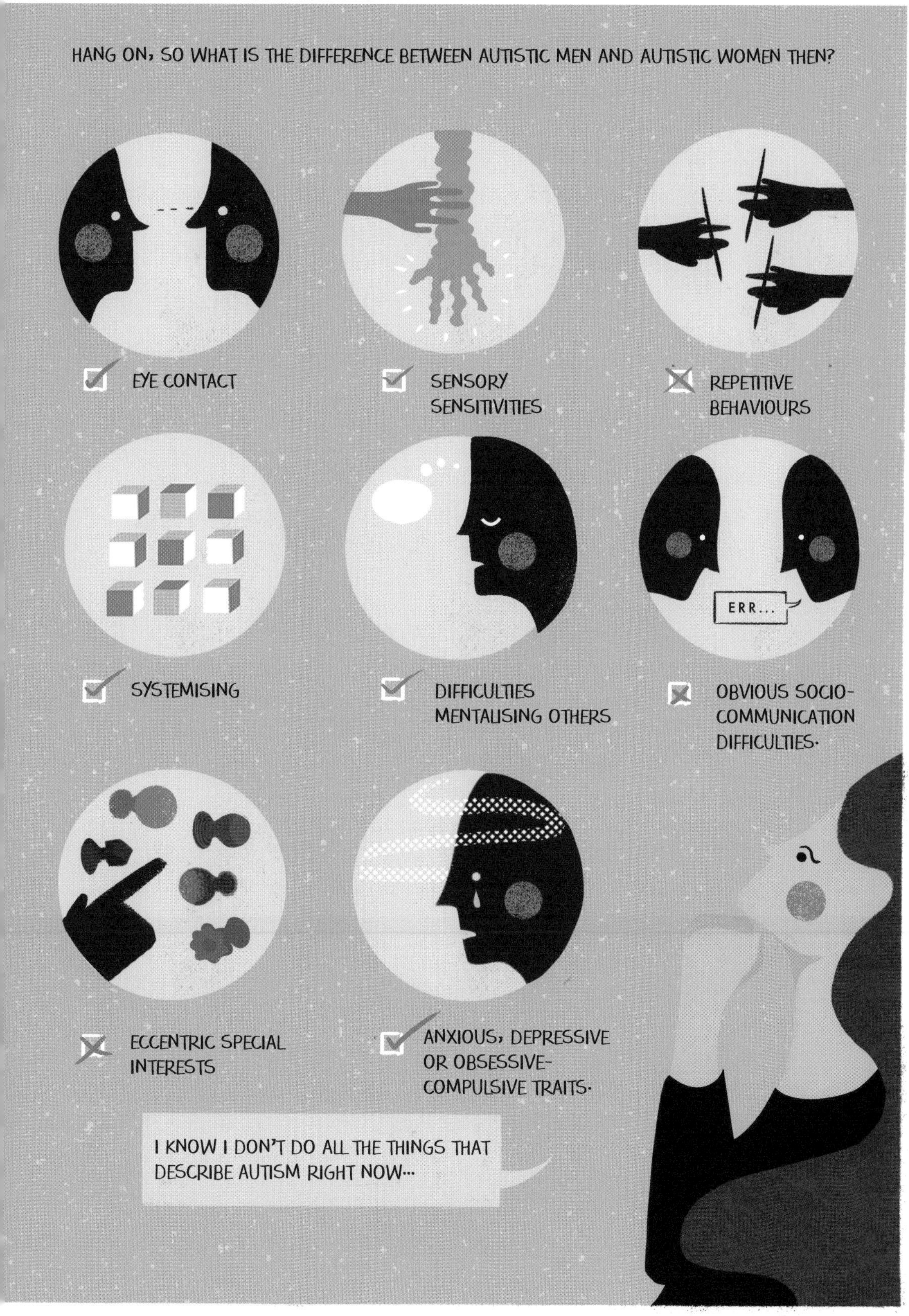
HANG ON, SO WHAT IS THE DIFFERENCE BETWEEN AUTISTIC MEN AND AUTISTIC WOMEN THEN?
EYE CONTACT
SENSORY SENSITIVITIES
REPETITIVE BEHAVIOURS
SYSTEMISING
DIFFICULTIES MENTALISING OTHERS
ERR...
OBVIOUS SOCIO-COMMUNICATION DIFFICULTIES.
ECCENTRIC SPECIAL INTERESTS
ANXIOUS, DEPRESSIVE OR OBSESSIVE-COMPULSIVE TRAITS.
I KNOW I DON'T DO ALL THE THINGS THAT DESCRIBE AUTISM RIGHT NOW...

SHE'S RIGHT, THE RESEARCH SHOWS:

BEHAVIOUR

♂   ♀

AUTISTIC WOMEN DISPLAY
FEWER REPETITIVE BEHAVIOURS
COMPARED TO AUTISTIC MEN.

IN SOCIAL SITUATIONS, AUTISTIC WOMEN A
MORE MOTIVATED TO SOCIALISE AND BETTE
AT MAKING FRIENDS COMPARED TO MEN.

AUTISTIC WOMEN ARE MORE LIKELY TO INTERNALISE (HIDE)
THEIR EMOTIONS, COMPARED TO AUTISTIC MEN WHO ARE
MORE LIKELY TO EXTERNALISE (SHOW) THEIR FEELINGS
AND SHOW THEIR ANGER OR DISAPPOINTMENT WITH A
SITUATION...

TO BETTER UNDERSTAND WHAT FEMALE AUTISM LOOKS LIKE, WE WILL HEAR STORIES DIRECTLY FROM THREE AUTISTIC WOMEN I INTERVIEWED...
THIS IS PAULA, SHE'S 24...
THIS IS ELLIE, SHE'S 19...
THIS IS MIMI, SHE'S 30...
I'VE ORGANISED THEIR STORIES INTO FOUR MAIN HEADLINES...

YOU'RE TOO POOR
AT MATHS TO BE
AUTISTIC

YOU'
JUS
A SH
GIR

THE FIRST HEADLINE IS:

YOU'RE NOT AUTISTIC

LOTS OF THE WOMEN TOLD ME THEY THOUGHT THEY HAD
AUTISM BUT WHEN THEY SUGGESTED IT TO FAMILY, FRIENDS
OR THEIR TEACHERS, IT WAS DISMISSED. WHEN THEY WENT
TO THEIR DOCTOR THEY WERE EITHER GIVEN THE WRONG
DIAGNOSIS OR TOLD THERE WAS NOTHING WRONG.

YOU ARE
ANXIOUS
NOT AUTIST

YOU'VE GOT
DEPRESSION, NOT
AUTISM!

E JUST
RENT

OF COURSE YOU'RE
NOT, YOU'RE JUST
KOOKY

YOU'
SOC
TO BE

YOU'VE GOT A
PERSONALITY
DISORDER

PRETENDING TO BE NORMAL

AS MANY WOMEN WEREN'T GIVEN A DIAGNOSIS AND THEY COULDN'T
UNDERSTAND WHY THEY WERE 'DIFFERENT', THEY TRIED TO 'FIT IN'
SOCIALLY, BY LEARNING TO BE LIKE OTHER GIRLS OR WOMEN IN
SOCIAL SITUATIONS.

FROM PASSIVE TO ASSERTIVE

MANY WOMEN TALKED ABOUT HOW THEIR IDENTITIES WERE BASED ON THEIR SPECIAL INTERESTS AND HOW THEY CAME TO EMBRACE THEIR DIAGNOSIS THROUGH FINDING A COMMUNITY OF FEMALES JUST LIKE THEM.

BEING SOCIALLY ISOLATED MEANT MANY WOMEN DIDN'T HAVE FEMALE FRIENDS AS TEENAGERS, WHERE INFORMAL RULES OF 'STAYING SAFE' WERE LEARNT. THIS MEANT THAT AUTISTIC WOMEN WERE ESPECIALLY VULNERABLE IN INTIMATE RELATIONSHIPS AND MANY WERE VICTIMS OF SEXUAL ABUSE. LATER THEY ALSO SHARED THEIR STORIES OF HOW THEY HAD LEARNT TO ASSERT THEMSELVES.

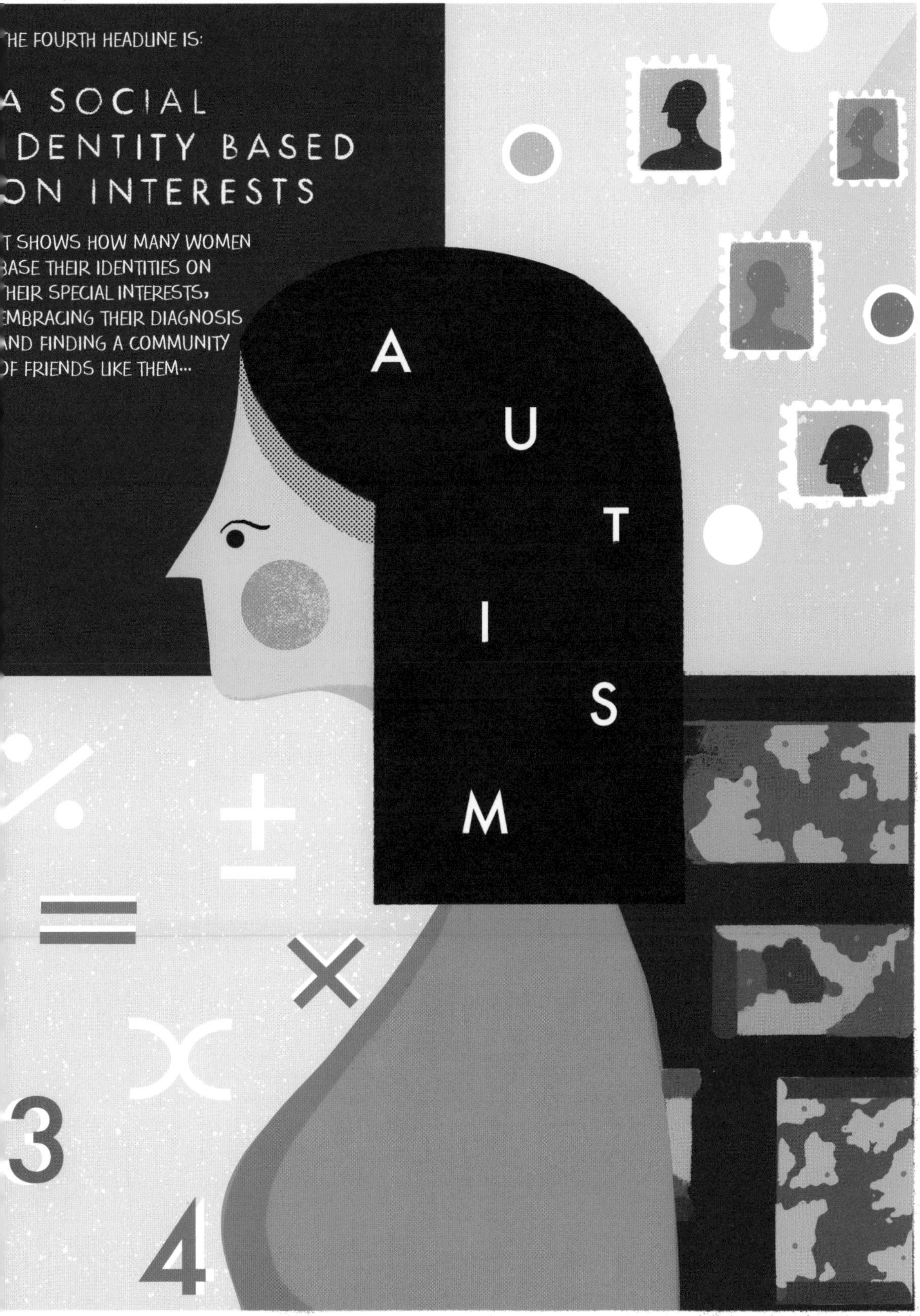
HE FOURTH HEADLINE IS:
A SOCIAL
DENTITY BASED
N INTERESTS
T SHOWS HOW MANY WOMEN
ASE THEIR IDENTITIES ON
HEIR SPECIAL INTERESTS,
MBRACING THEIR DIAGNOSIS
ND FINDING A COMMUNITY
F FRIENDS LIKE THEM...
AUTISM
3
4

SO, LET'S START WITH THE HEADLINE 'YOU'RE NOT AUTISTIC'. WHAT ARE YOUR EXPERIENCES OF THIS?

"IN MY FAMILY, WE JOKINGLY GAVE EACH OTHER LABELS – I WAS THE 'AUTISTIC ONE' AND MY SISTER WAS THE 'BOSSY ONE'. WHEN I ASKED MY MUM IF SHE THOUGHT I WAS AUTISTIC, SHE LAUGHED AND SAID, 'OF COURSE NOT, YOU'RE JUST MIMI.' I DID MY RESEARCH ON AUTISM ON THE INTERNET AND WENT TO THE DOCTOR TO SEE IF I COULD GET A DIAGNOSIS. BUT I WAS JUST TOLD I WAS ANXIOUS AND WAS PRESCRIBED MEDICATION."

"WHEN A SPECIAL NEEDS TEACHER CAME TO ASSESS ME, HE SAID, 'YOU CAN'T BE AUTISTIC, YOU'RE NOT GOOD ENOUGH AT MATHS.' I THINK HE HAD THIS 'RAIN MAN' STEREOTYPE IN HIS HEAD, WHICH I DIDN'T FIT."

"I WAS TOLD 'ALL GIRLS LIKE PONIES, THAT'S NOT A SPECIAL INTEREST!' WHICH WASN'T TRUE. I KNEW FAR MORE ABOUT PONIES THAN ANYONE ELSE IN THE RIDING SCHOOL. I ALSO LOVED COLLECTING THINGS, MY BIGGEST COLLECTION BEING MY BOTTLE TOPS…"

HOW WAS SCHOOL?
"I REMEMBER BEING REALLY QUIET AT PRIMARY SCHOOL. I WAS PERFECT, DID EVERYTHING I WAS TOLD AND BOTTLED EVERYTHING UP. BUT WHEN I GOT HOME I WOULD EXPLODE – I'D JUST SPENT THE WHOLE DAY HOLDING EVERYTHING IN."

"SAME. SECONDARY SCHOOL WAS DIFFICULT... I REMEMBER ONE TIME, IN A MATHS LESSON I YAWNED, AND THE TEACHER ASKED, 'IS THIS LESSON BORING YOU?' AND I SAID 'YES, MISS', AND SHE GAVE ME A DETENTION! I WAS REALLY UPSET, I DIDN'T SEE WHAT I HAD DONE WRONG. SHE HAD ASKED ME A QUESTION AND I HAD ANSWERED IT TRUTHFULLY. MY CLASSMATES TRIED TO EXPLAIN TO ME, 'YOU SHOULDN'T SAY THAT, IT'S RUDE.' I GET IT NOW, BUT I STILL DON'T SEE THE LOGIC BEHIND IT EVEN THOUGH I CAN SEE I MUSTN'T DO IT!"

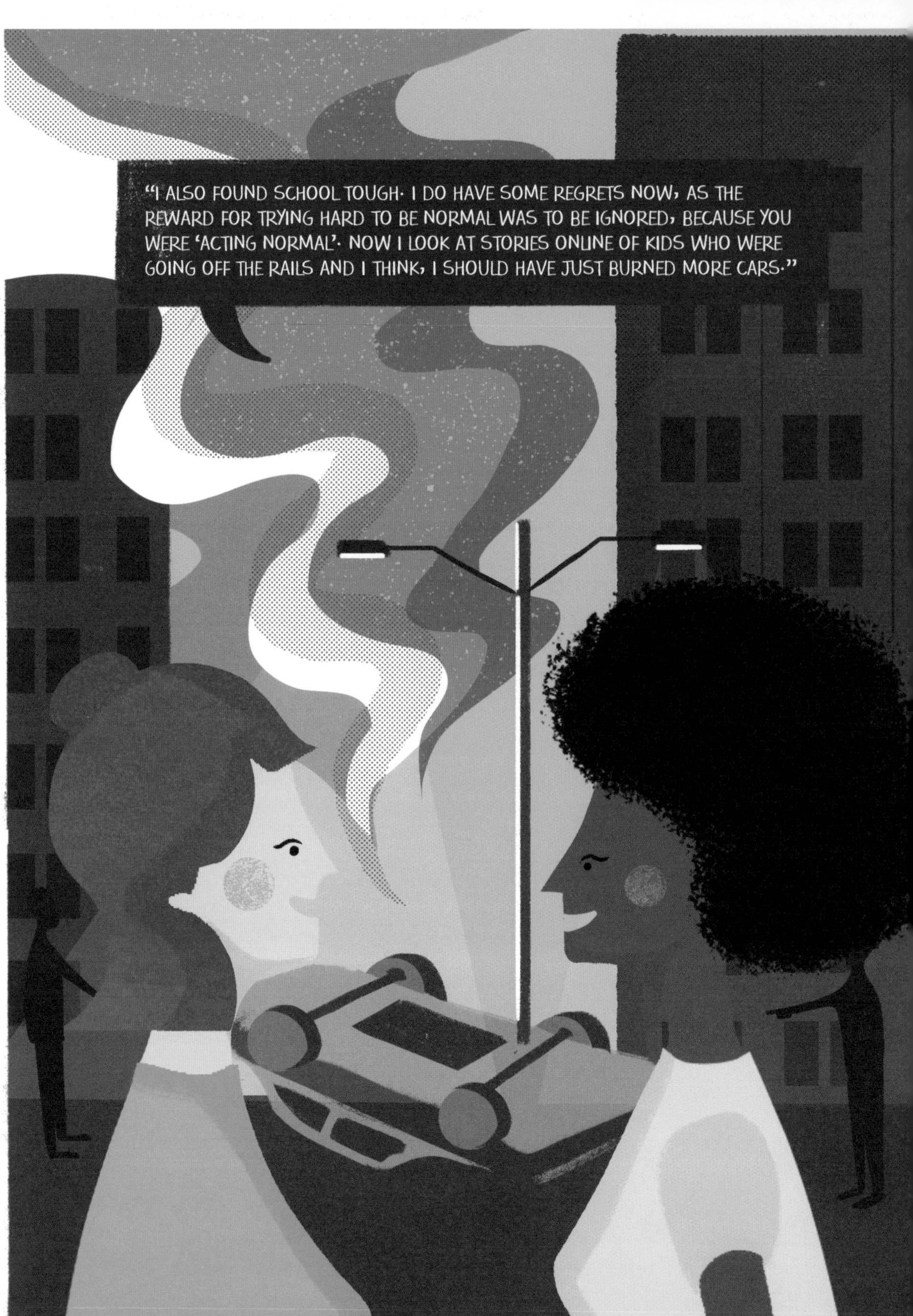
"I ALSO FOUND SCHOOL TOUGH. I DO HAVE SOME REGRETS NOW, AS THE REWARD FOR TRYING HARD TO BE NORMAL WAS TO BE IGNORED, BECAUSE YOU WERE 'ACTING NORMAL'. NOW I LOOK AT STORIES ONLINE OF KIDS WHO WERE GOING OFF THE RAILS AND I THINK, I SHOULD HAVE JUST BURNED MORE CARS."

"THERE'S THIS BOOK BY ELLEN MONTGOMERY AND THE CHARACTER EMILY, WHENEVER SOMEBODY IS HORRIBLE TO HER SHE JUST LOOKS AT THEM, AND BECAUSE OF HER EXPRESSION THEY GO AWAY. IMAGINE MY SHOCK WHEN IT DIDN'T WORK WHEN I WAS BEING BULLIED.

SOMETIMES IT WENT REALLY BADLY BECAUSE THE BOOKS I READ WERE A FEW HUNDRED YEARS OLD AND I WOULD QUOTE DIRECTLY FROM THEM AND IT DIDN'T SOUND RIGHT, BUT I COULDN'T SEE THAT. I SAW THAT THIS CHARACTER HAD HAD A CERTAIN IMPACT – BY SAYING A CERTAIN THING HE'D GOT PEOPLE WHO WERE BOTHERING HIM TO GO AWAY AND I WANTED TO DO THAT TOO…"

'AWAY YOU STARVELLING, YOU ELF-SKIN, YOU DRIED NEAT'S-TONGUE, BULL'S-PIZZLE, YOU STOCK FISH!'[6]

ry IV Part 1 (Act 2, Scene 4).

"FOR ME, IT WAS AUTOMATIC, I'LL MIMIC WHAT OTHER PEOPLE ARE DOING OR SAYING OR THEIR ACCENTS WITHOUT NOTICING. I USED TO GO CAMPING WITH GIRL GUIDES AND COME BACK WITH STRONG ACCENTS. ONE TIME I CAME BACK WITH AN IRISH ACCENT AND IT TOOK A WEEK TO GET RID OF IT…"

"THAT'S FUNNY, I WAS MORE CONSCIOUS OF TRYING TO 'FIT IN'. I HONED SOMETHING OF A PERSONA WHICH WAS BUBBLY AND MAYBE A BIT DIM, BECAUSE I HAD NOTHING TO TALK ABOUT AT PARTIES OTHER THAN CREATIVE WRITING. SO, I CULTIVATED AN IMAGE THAT I BROUGHT OUT TO SOCIAL SITUATIONS THAT WAS NOT 'ME'. AFTERWARDS, I WAS EXHAUSTED; IT'S A MASSIVE EFFORT HAVING TO PLAY SOMEONE ELSE. I HAD TO GO AND LIE DOWN IN A ROOM ALONE TO RECOVER."

WERE THERE ANY
DISADVANTAGES TO MASKING?

"WELL, I WAS SO GOOD AT ACTING
NEUROTYPICAL SO CONVINCINGLY
THAT I WONDERED WHETHER I HAD
AUTISM AT ALL···"

```
@conversation

// command: listen to other person        // display: open body language
//: wait until they finish                 // command: ask questions
// command: [smile] talk back              // := friendship
```

"IT'S VERY DRAINING TRYING TO FIGURE
OUT EVERYTHING ALL THE TIME, EVERYTHING
IS MORE LIKE ON A MANUAL, YOU'VE GOT
TO USE ONE OF THOSE COMPUTERS WHERE
YOU HAVE TO TYPE EVERY COMMAND IN·"

Why are they
talking like that?

They're having a
nice time...

?

THE THIRD HEADLINE DESCRIBES WOMEN'S
JOURNEYS 'FROM PASSIVE TO ASSERTIVE'.

MANY WOMEN DESCRIBED THEMSELVES
AS 'PASSIVE' OR 'CONFLICT-AVOIDANT'.
THEY PREFERRED TO AGREE IN SOCIAL
SITUATIONS BECAUSE THEY WEREN'T
SURE OF THE SOCIAL RULES, OFTEN
LEARNING THEM BY TRIAL AND ERROR.

ON THE WHOLE THIS STRATEGY WORKED, BUT IN THE WORLD OF DATING AND
INTIMATE RELATIONSHIPS, IT HAD POTENTIAL TO GO WRONG. HOWEVER,
MANY LEARNT TO ASSERT THEMSELVES AFTER HAVING OVERCOME DIFFICULT
EXPERIENCES.

The
perfect
Girlfriend

"I ALMOST FEEL PRESSURED BY SOCIETY TO
HAVE SEX BECAUSE YOU GET TOLD THIS IS
WHAT IS EXPECTED OF YOU TO BE A GOOD
GIRLFRIEND AND YOU THINK, 'IF I DON'T DO
IT, THEN I AM NOT FULFILLING MY DUTIES.'"

"IN RELATIONSHIPS IT WAS DIFFICULT, BECAUSE NO ONE EVER TELLS YOU THE RULES, OR WHAT IS APPROPRIATE OR NOT. I KNEW I WAS TAKEN ADVANTAGE OF MANY TIMES. YOU JUST ASSUME PEOPLE ARE TELLING YOU THE TRUTH…"

THE TIME, I THOUGHT, HE MUST HAVE BEEN ABLE
REGISTER THAT I WASN'T KEEN BECAUSE I KEPT
NG TO BREAK UP WITH HIM. BUT WHENEVER I
HE WOULD SAY I WAS MAKING A MISTAKE OR I
N'T KNOW MY OWN FEELINGS, AND I WAS AT MY
'S END, I FELT SO TRAPPED."

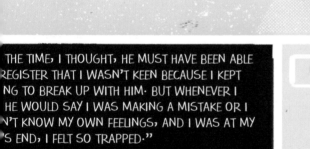

I'M SORRY, YOU'RE RIGHT

I DON'T MIND, WE CAN DO IT IF YOU WANT TO

SURE,
LET'S DO IT YOUR WAY

"I REMEMBER BEING WITHDRAWN. THERE WAS A SENSE OF APPEASING: 'PLEASE, APPEASE AND APOLOGISE.'"

WHAT CHANGED AS A RESULT OF THESE EXPERIENCES?

"I THINK THE BIG THING FOR ME WAS LEARNING I COULD SAY NO. I HADN'T KNOWN THAT BEFORE. I HAD LEARNT THIS RULE TO BE RESPECTFUL TO YOUR ELDERS AND APPLIED IT EVERYWHERE. BUT AFTER LEARNING I COULD SAY NO, THERE WERE TIMES WHEN GUYS PUSHED FOR IT AND I JUST WALKED AWAY."

NO

"IT'S HARD TO COME ACROSS AT THE RIGHT LEVE SOMETIMES THOUGH. I KNOW SOMETIMES WHEN FINALLY SAY WHAT I WANT AND MEAN, I CAN BE A BIT TOO BLUNT..."

"WE NOW HAVE A WOMEN'S GROUP AND I'M THE RELATIONSHIP EXPERT IN THE GROUP. THE WOMEN WILL COME TO TALK TO ME ABOUT THINGS, ASK FOR ADVICE, HOW TO MEET PEOPLE ONLINE. I KNOW ALL THE RULES, BECAUSE I'VE GONE THROUGH IT..."

THE FINAL HEADLINE, 'A SOCIAL IDENTITY BASED ON INTERESTS', EXPLORES
THE ROLE THAT FRIENDSHIPS PLAYED IN HELPING WOMEN DEFINE THEMSELVES
AND BETTER UNDERSTAND THEIR AUTISM.

EN I CAME ACROSS THIS AUTISM BLOG POST,
CH SAID 'IT'S A DIFFERENCE NOT A DISORDER',
AS SO HELPFUL TO FRAME IT IN THAT WAY; IT
T MADE ME FEEL GOOD ABOUT MYSELF."

"YEAH, I FOUND FORUMS ONLINE HUGELY
SUPPORTIVE. THAT'S WHERE I MET A GANG OF
FELLOW ASPIE WOMEN, THEY ARE NOW PEOPLE
I THINK OF AS MY FAMILY."

"SOMETHING THAT I REALLY APPRECIATE ABOUT HAVING A DIAGNOSIS IS ACTUALLY
BEING IN THIS CLUB NOW WHERE PEOPLE TALK ABOUT THEIR EXPERIENCES THAT HAVE
SO MANY ECHOES OF MY OWN."

"ALSO, JUST USING A COMPUTER TO COMMUNICATE RELIEVES LOADS OF PRESSURE AROUND SOCIAL COMMUNICATION. YOU DON'T HAVE TO THINK ABOUT BODY LANGUAGE OR FACIAL EXPRESSIONS OR RESPONDING STRAIGHT AWAY. ALL YOU HAVE IS THE TEXT YOU ARE TYPING FOR EACH OTHER AND IT FEELS COMPLETELY EQUAL. ALSO, IT'S MUCH EASIER TO TALK ABOUT YOUR EMOTIONS WHEN TYPING!"

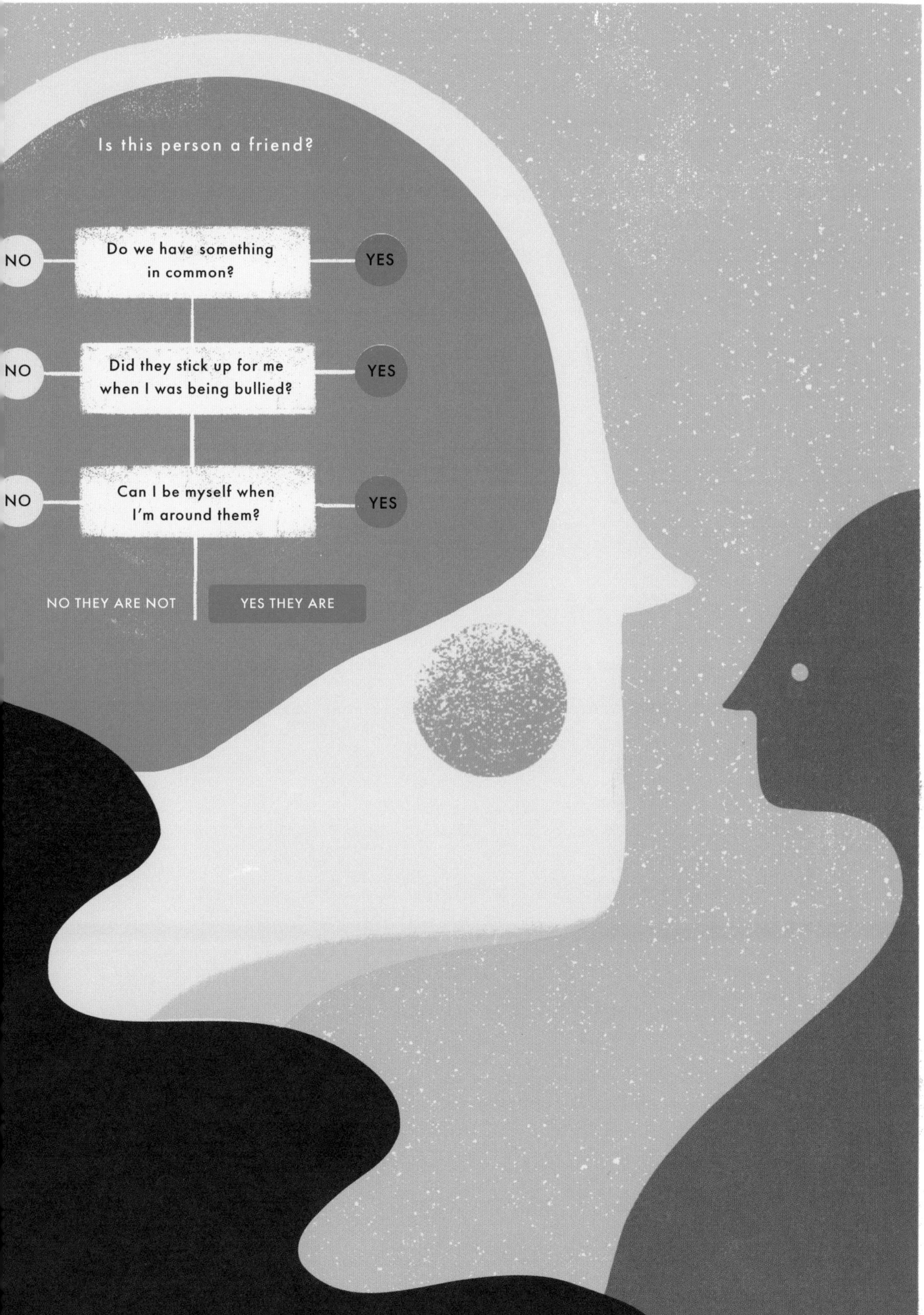
Is this person a friend?
NO
Do we have something in common?
YES
NO
Did they stick up for me when I was being bullied?
YES
NO
Can I be myself when I'm around them?
YES
NO THEY ARE NOT
YES THEY ARE

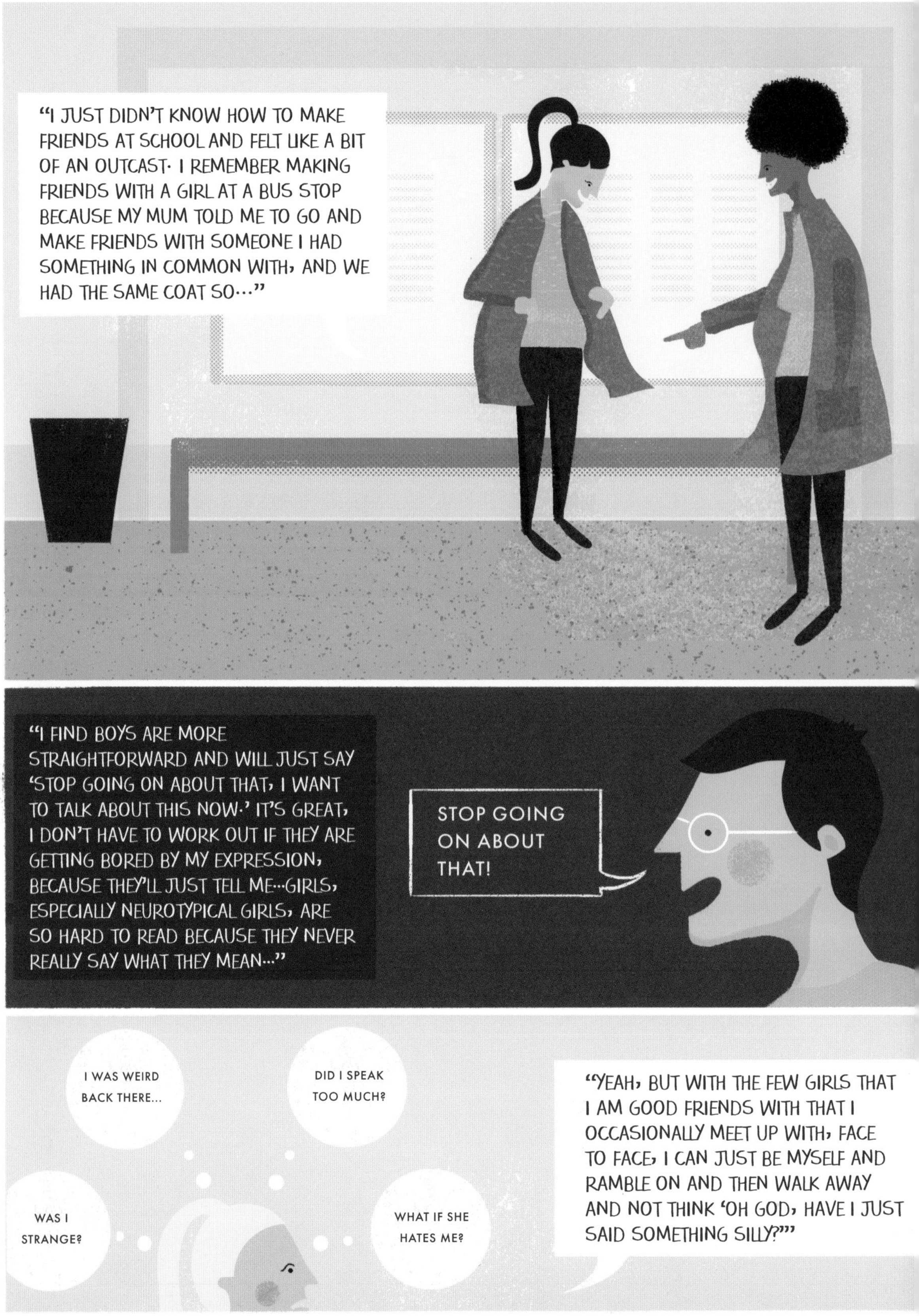
"I JUST DIDN'T KNOW HOW TO MAKE FRIENDS AT SCHOOL AND FELT LIKE A BIT OF AN OUTCAST. I REMEMBER MAKING FRIENDS WITH A GIRL AT A BUS STOP BECAUSE MY MUM TOLD ME TO GO AND MAKE FRIENDS WITH SOMEONE I HAD SOMETHING IN COMMON WITH, AND WE HAD THE SAME COAT SO..."
"I FIND BOYS ARE MORE STRAIGHTFORWARD AND WILL JUST SAY 'STOP GOING ON ABOUT THAT, I WANT TO TALK ABOUT THIS NOW.' IT'S GREAT, I DON'T HAVE TO WORK OUT IF THEY ARE GETTING BORED BY MY EXPRESSION, BECAUSE THEY'LL JUST TELL ME...GIRLS, ESPECIALLY NEUROTYPICAL GIRLS, ARE SO HARD TO READ BECAUSE THEY NEVER REALLY SAY WHAT THEY MEAN..."
STOP GOING ON ABOUT THAT!
I WAS WEIRD BACK THERE...
DID I SPEAK TOO MUCH?
WAS I STRANGE?
WHAT IF SHE HATES ME?
"YEAH, BUT WITH THE FEW GIRLS THAT I AM GOOD FRIENDS WITH THAT I OCCASIONALLY MEET UP WITH, FACE TO FACE, I CAN JUST BE MYSELF AND RAMBLE ON AND THEN WALK AWAY AND NOT THINK 'OH GOD, HAVE I JUST SAID SOMETHING SILLY?'"

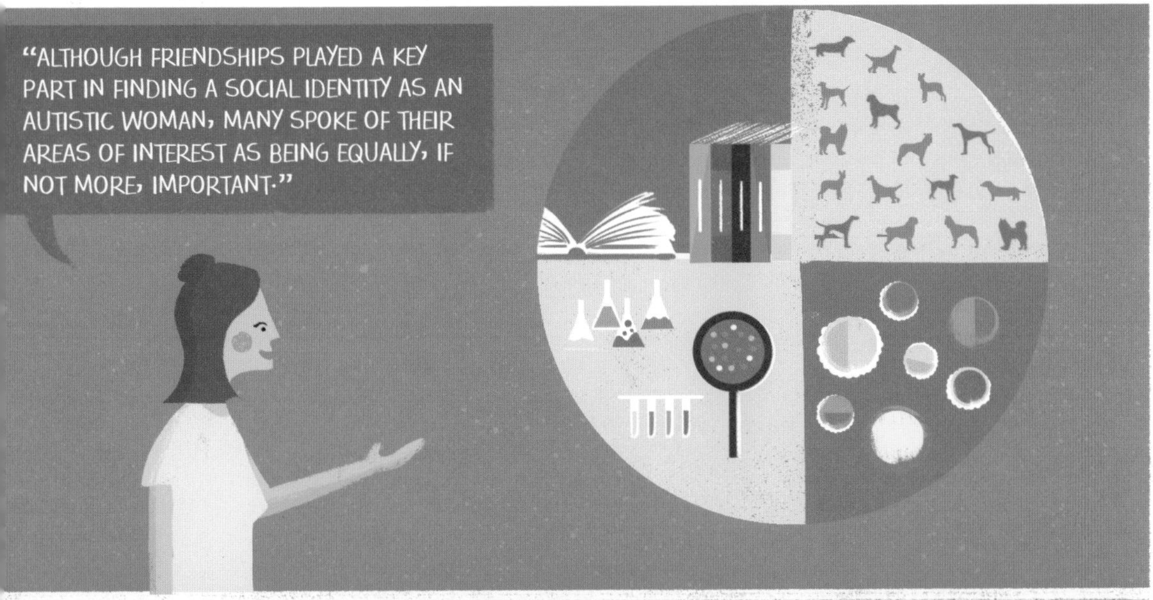
"ALTHOUGH FRIENDSHIPS PLAYED A KEY PART IN FINDING A SOCIAL IDENTITY AS AN AUTISTIC WOMAN, MANY SPOKE OF THEIR AREAS OF INTEREST AS BEING EQUALLY, IF NOT MORE, IMPORTANT."

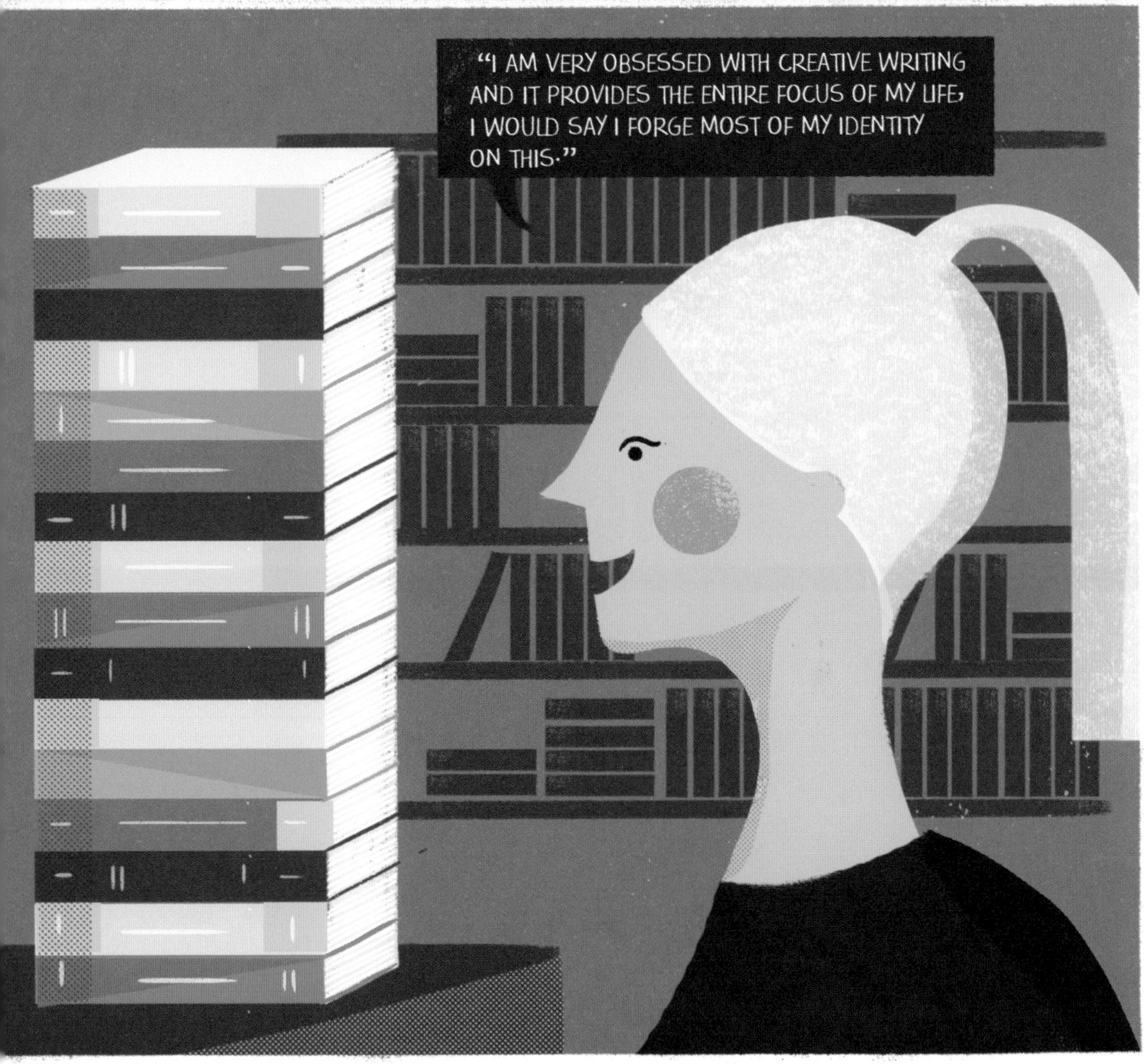
"I AM VERY OBSESSED WITH CREATIVE WRITING AND IT PROVIDES THE ENTIRE FOCUS OF MY LIFE, I WOULD SAY I FORGE MOST OF MY IDENTITY ON THIS."

"I'M REALLY INTO BIPLANES AND VINTAGE AIRCRAFTS. IT ALL STARTED FROM AN IDEA FOR A STORY I WANTED TO WRITE AND ILLUSTRATE ABOUT A FEMALE CHARTERED PILOT…THEN I WANTED TO LEARN HOW TO DRAW A BIPLANE. I'VE NOW LEARNT HOW TO IDENTIFY PLANES BY SIGHT, HAVING READ ABOUT HOW THEY WERE USED, AND ALSO GOT REALLY INTO WORLD WAR ONE…NOW EVERY TIME THAT I SEE A BIPLANE IT FILLS ME WITH SO MUCH JOY."

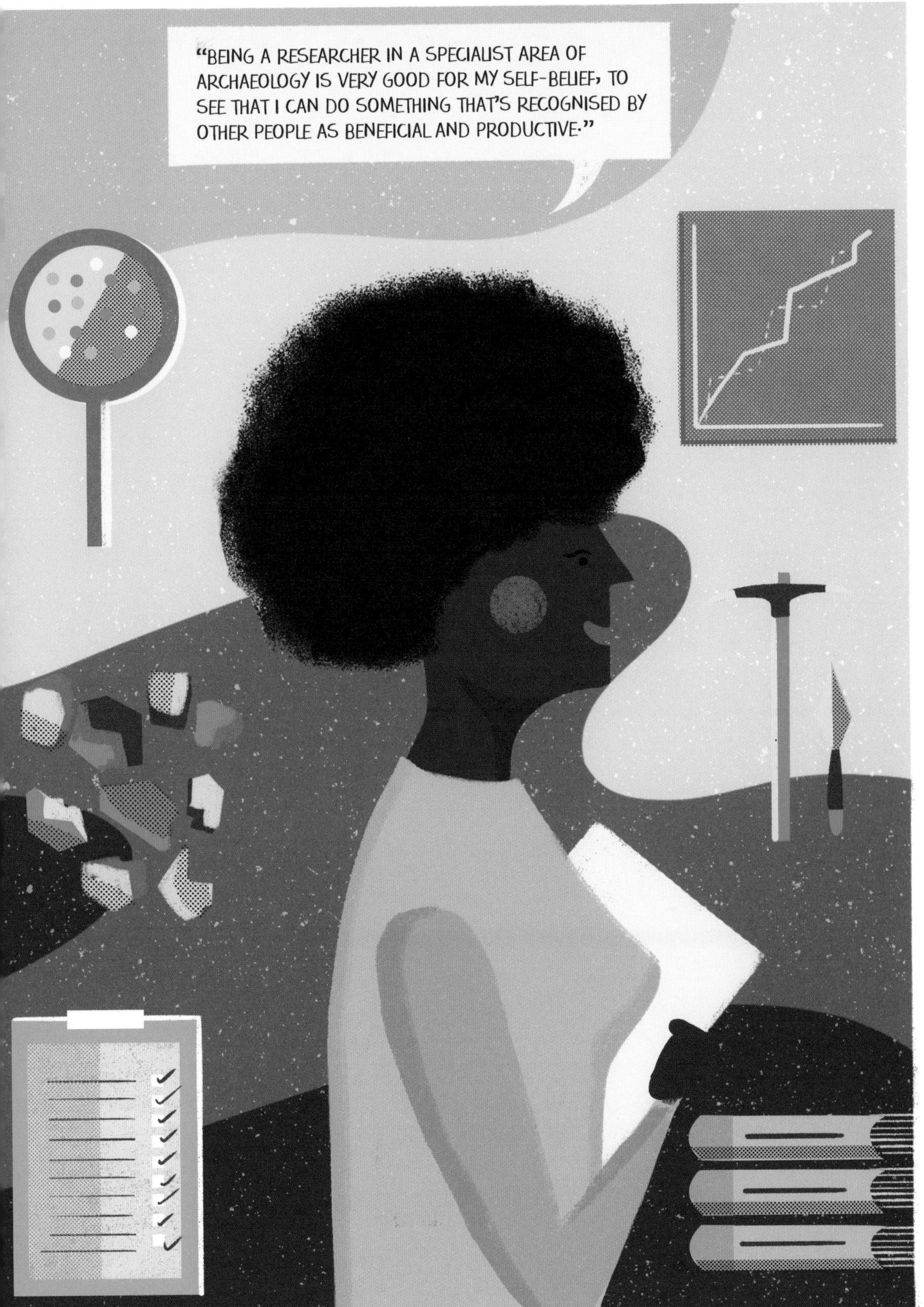
"BEING A RESEARCHER IN A SPECIALIST AREA OF ARCHAEOLOGY IS VERY GOOD FOR MY SELF-BELIEF, TO SEE THAT I CAN DO SOMETHING THAT'S RECOGNISED BY OTHER PEOPLE AS BENEFICIAL AND PRODUCTIVE."

"WITH MY ASPERGER'S THERE ARE ALWAYS A MILLION THINGS IN MY HEAD, BUT WHEN I'M IN A BOAT I CAN JUST FOCUS ON BEING IN A BOAT. IT'S THE ONLY PLACE I EVER GET THE SENSATION OF FEELING CALM… ASPERGER'S IS TIRING BECAUSE IT'S ALMOST LIKE YOU'RE ON HIGH ALERT ALL THE TIME, SO TO BE AT PEACE AND NOT CONSTANTLY FEEL ON THE EDGE OF A MELTDOWN IS GREAT."

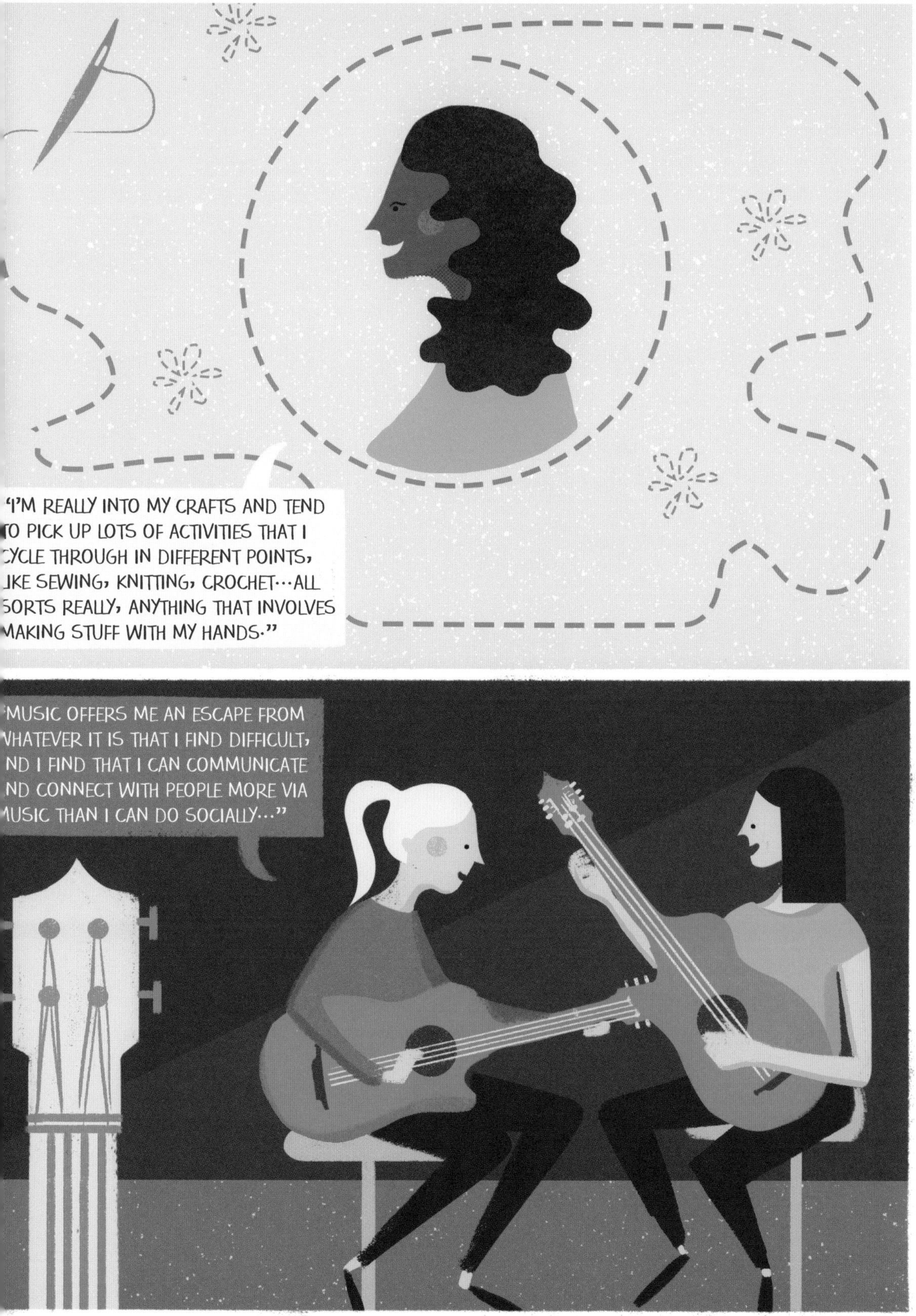

"I'M REALLY INTO MY CRAFTS AND TEND TO PICK UP LOTS OF ACTIVITIES THAT I CYCLE THROUGH IN DIFFERENT POINTS, LIKE SEWING, KNITTING, CROCHET…ALL SORTS REALLY, ANYTHING THAT INVOLVES MAKING STUFF WITH MY HANDS."
"MUSIC OFFERS ME AN ESCAPE FROM WHATEVER IT IS THAT I FIND DIFFICULT, ND I FIND THAT I CAN COMMUNICATE ND CONNECT WITH PEOPLE MORE VIA MUSIC THAN I CAN DO SOCIALLY…"

SO, NOW WE KNOW A LITTLE MORE ABOUT WHAT MIGHT BE DIFFERENT BETWEEN MALE AND FEMALE AUTISM, WHAT'S NEXT IN THE WORLD OF RESEARCH?

FEMALE

MORE SENSORY SENSITIVITIES

FEWER STEREOTYPED BEHAVIOURS

SHOW FEWER AND ARE MORE AWARE OF THEIR AUTISTIC TRAITS

SPECIAL INTERESTS

FEWER SOCIO-COMMUNICATION DIFFICULTIES

CAMOUFLAGING

LAI AND COLLEAGUES (2016) FOUND THAT AUTISTIC WOMEN'S ABILITY TO CAMOUFLAGE HAS ALSO BEEN NOTED IN AUTISTIC MEN AND NON-BINARY INDIVIDUALS.

MENTAL HEALTH

CAGE'S (2017) RESEARCH TEAM ALSO REPORTED THAT CAMOUFLAGING IS A STRONG PREDICTOR OF SUICIDE IN AUTISM.

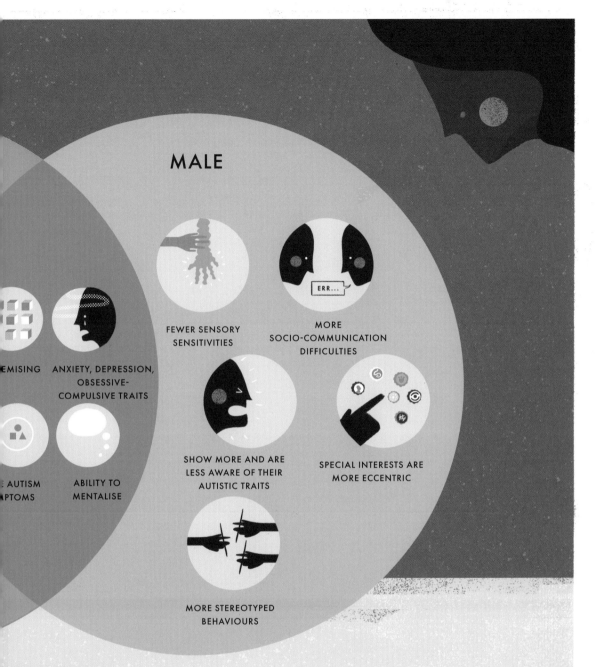

MALE

FEWER SENSORY
SENSITIVITIES

MORE
SOCIO-COMMUNICATION
DIFFICULTIES

...EMISING

ANXIETY, DEPRESSION,
OBSESSIVE-
COMPULSIVE TRAITS

SHOW MORE AND ARE
LESS AWARE OF THEIR
AUTISTIC TRAITS

SPECIAL INTERESTS ARE
MORE ECCENTRIC

...E AUTISM
...PTOMS

ABILITY TO
MENTALISE

MORE STEREOTYPED
BEHAVIOURS

DIAGNOSTIC TOOLS

LONGITUDINAL RESEARCH BY JENSEN'S
DANISH TEAM (2014) IS ALSO LOOKING
TO TEST WHETHER THE QUESTIONNAIRES
USED TO DIAGNOSE AUTISM MIGHT BE
BIASED AGAINST WOMEN AND IS TRYING
TO DEVELOP MORE SENSITIVE TOOLS THAT
CAPTURE BOTH MALE AND FEMALE AUTISM.

SHARING THE KNOWLEDGE THAT AUTISM
EVEN EXISTS IN FEMALES IS IMPORTANT FOR
CHALLENGING COMMON BIASES AND BELIEFS.
THIS WAY, AUTISTIC GIRLS AND WOMEN CAN
BE SAFE, RECOGNISED AND CELEBRATED FOR
THEIR DIFFERENCES. SO ONCE YOU'VE READ
THIS, PASS IT ON!

FURTHER READING

REFERENCES

CAGE, E., DI MONACO, J., & NEWELL, V. (2017) EXPERIENCES OF AUTISM ACCEPTANCE AND MENTAL HEALTH IN AUTISTIC ADULTS. *JOURNAL OF AUTISM AND DEVELOPMENTAL DISORDERS*, 5-8.

LAI, M-C., LOMBARDO, M.V., RUIGROK, A.N.V., CHAKRABARTI, B., *ET AL*. (2017) QUANTIFYING AND EXPLORING CAMOUFLAGING IN MEN AND WOMEN WITH AUTISM. *AUTISM*, 21(6), 690-702.

JENSEN C.M., STEINHAUSEN H.C., & LAURITSEN, M.B. (2014) TIME TRENDS OVER 16 YEARS IN INCIDENCE-RATES OF AUTISM SPECTRUM DISORDERS ACROSS THE LIFESPAN BASED ON NATIONWIDE DANISH REGISTER DATA. *JOURNAL OF AUTISM AND DEVELOPMENTAL DISORDERS*, 44(8), 1808-1818.

BOOKS

THINKING IN PICTURES: MY LIFE WITH AUTISM BY TEMPLE GRANDIN

ALL CATS HAVE ASPERGER SYNDROME BY KATHY HOOPMANN

LA DIFFÉRENCE INVISIBLE BY JULIE DACHEZ AND MADEMOISELLE CAROLINE

WEBSITES

THEGIRLWITHTHECURLYHAIR.CO.UK

ROBYNSTEWARD.COM

PROJECTS

PEOPLELIKEUS.DK
PEOPLE LIKE US IS A DANISH BREWING COMPANY, RUN BY AUTISTS

FIRST PUBLISHED IN 2019
BY JESSICA KINGSLEY PUBLISHERS
73 COLLIER STREET
LONDON N1 9BE, UK
AND
400 MARKET STREET, SUITE 400
PHILADELPHIA, PA 19106, USA

WWW.JKP.COM

LIBRARY OF CONGRESS CATALOGING IN PUBLICATION DATA

ISBN 978 1 78592 566 5
EISBN 978 1 78592 667 9

PRINTED AND BOUND IN CHINA

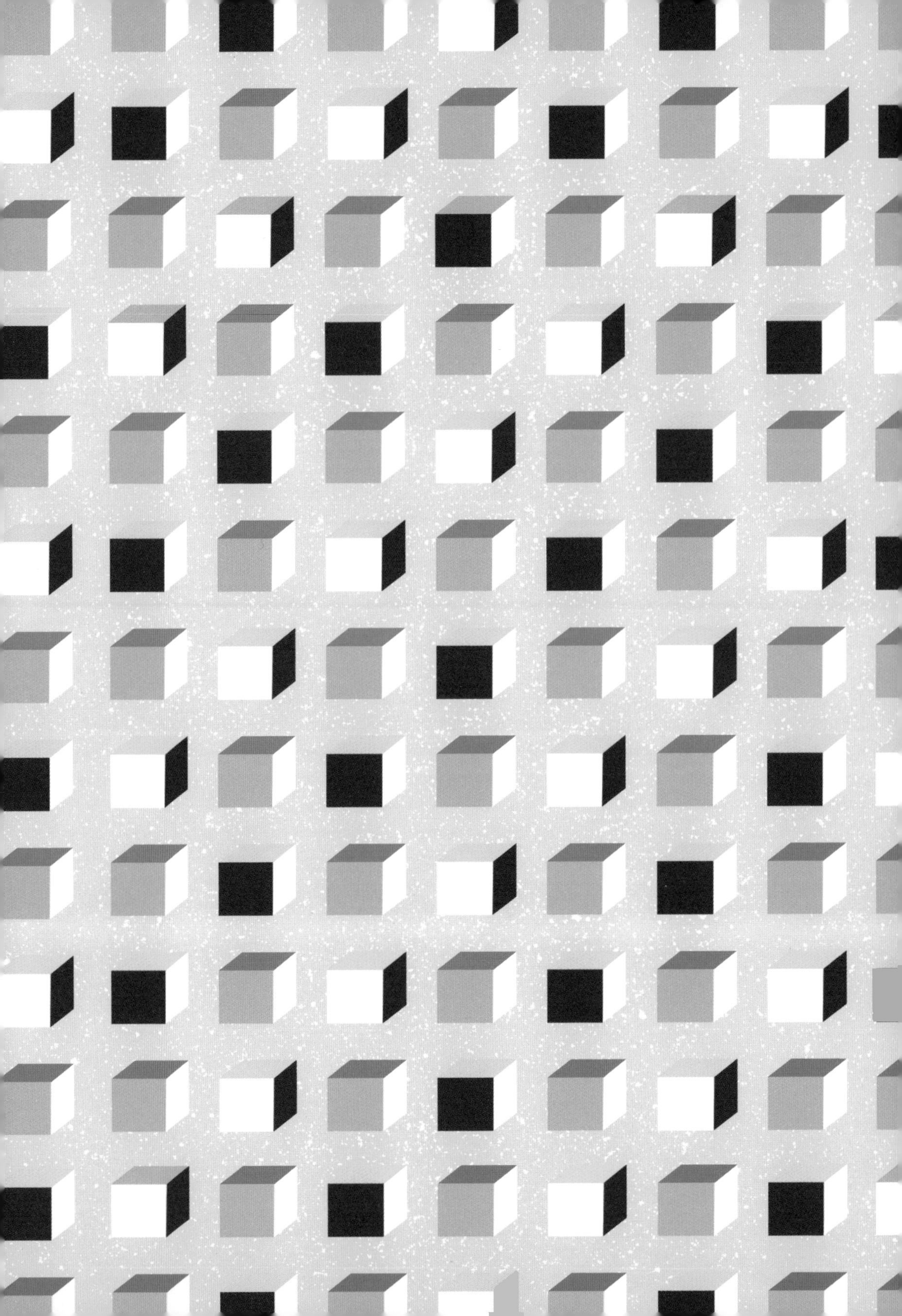